Original title:

The Inner Labyrinth

Author: Olivia Oja

ISBN HARDBACK: 978-1-80561-052-6

ISBN PAPERBACK: 978-1-80561-613-9

The Enigmatic Interior

Shadows dance along the wall,
Whispers echo, softly call.
Secrets lie in corners deep,
Where ancient memories still sleep.

Fragrant roses hide the thorns,
Ghosts of laughter, hearts now worn.
Every room a tale to tell,
In silence, stories cast their spell.

Mirrors reflect a past unbound,
Depths of sorrow can be found.
Light flickers, a fleeting beam,
Unveiling truth in fragile dream.

Worn-out books with pages torn,
In the stillness, solace born.
Puzzles weave in dusty light,
Navigating gloom and sight.

Here within this quiet space,
Time stands still, a gentle grace.
Lost in thought, we may discover,
The depths that pull us, one another.

Colors of Contemplation

Brush of blue on canvas wide,
Whispers of the heart abide.
Crimson dreams soothe weary minds,
In each stroke, a truth that binds.

Sunset fades, the sky ablaze,
A tranquil moment, thoughts do graze.
Emerald glimmers, nature's sigh,
Colors merge, as shadows fly.

Golden hues of memories past,
Time flows by, yet love will last.
A palette rich with joy and pain,
In silence, wisdom's golden grain.

Purple hues awaken dusk,
In the quiet, peace we trust.
Each shade a feeling to embrace,
In reflection, we find our place.

In this realm of vibrant hue,
Contemplations, fresh and new.
With every layer, life unfolds,
A story painted, bright and bold.

Navigating the Inward Sea

Waves of thought crash on the mind,
Echoes of the soul entwined.
Sailing forth on currents deep,
In silence, hidden treasures keep.

Rhythms shift as tides do turn,
In waters still, we seek and learn.
Compass set to dreams untold,
In the storm, our courage bold.

Stormy winds, navigating fears,
In the depths, we confront tears.
Each swell a lesson, ride the flow,
Inward journey, let love grow.

Stars above, they guide our way,
Through the night, they softly sway.
As we traverse this ocean wide,
In the heart, our truths abide.

Anchor down, we pause to breathe,
In the stillness, we believe.
Navigating the inward sea,
In ourselves, we set us free.

Cracks in the Facade

Quiet whispers through the walls,
Secrets hide where silence calls.
Painted smiles, yet shadows lie,
In the light, the truth might cry.

Each scratch tells a story old,
Of broken dreams and hearts of gold.
In the cracks, we often see,
Beauty found in what can't be.

Windows cracked, a glimpse of soul,
In imperfections, we feel whole.
Echoes linger in the air,
For every loss, a hidden care.

Behind the guise, a heart that bleeds,
In every fracture, love's own seeds.
Facades crumble, yet we grow,
Through the fissures, life will flow.

With each flaw, a tale unfolds,
In the cracks, what time upholds.
Embrace the scars, let them show,
For within them, we find the glow.

Maze of Thoughts

In corridors of dreams I stray,
Whispers linger, hidden ways.
Turning left and feeling lost,
Navigating at what cost?

Flickering lights reflect my fears,
Silent shadows dance with tears.
Every turn, a choice to make,
Crucial paths begin to shake.

Fragments of a distant time,
Captured echoes, lost in rhyme.
Winding routes, a tangled thread,
Leading to the words unsaid.

Each step I take, the walls confine,
Embracing darkness, seeking shine.
Where do I end, where do I start?
A labyrinth forged within my heart.

Echoes in the Mind

Thoughts resound like distant chimes,
Drifting softly through the climes.
Memories replay, shadows cast,
Fleeting moments, fading fast.

Voices linger in the haze,
Familiar tunes, a haunting phase.
Words unspoken fill the air,
A silent song, a whispered prayer.

Time loops back on itself, it seems,
Cradling fragments of lost dreams.
Chasing echoes through the night,
Glancing shadows, seeking light.

Patterns weave in shades of gray,
In the silence, ghosts will play.
Navigating through the unseen,
In the echoes, I've always been.

Twisting Passageways

Winding paths that twist and turn,
In the silence, lessons learn.
Crossroads beckon with their charm,
Yet fear lingers, cold and warm.

Each step forward, doubt prevails,
Silent whispers, soft exhale.
In the dark, a flicker glows,
Guiding me where the river flows.

Walls of memories shift and sway,
Holding secrets in their play.
Every twist, a tale to tell,
In this maze, I know so well.

Reflections dance in candlelight,
Drawing me into the night.
Every passage leads to grace,
Searching for my sacred place.

Reflections in Shadow

In the twilight, shadows creep,
Silent moments, secrets keep.
Faces blur, yet hearts define,
In the dark, a spark does shine.

Echoes whisper on the breeze,
Tales of longing, memories tease.
Underneath the quiet gloom,
Hope ignites, dispelling doom.

Layers fall, revealing light,
Painting colors in the night.
Reflections dance upon the wall,
Fragile beauty, standing tall.

In these shadows, dreams awake,
Fears dissolve, new paths we take.
Through the dusk, we find our way,
In shadows deep, we learn to stay.

Curved Echoes

In the quiet of the night,
Whispers dance beneath the stars.
Softly tracing memories' flight,
Curved echoes from afar.

Leaves rustle like gentle sighs,
Carried by the moonlit breeze.
Time uncurls, and softly flies,
Binding moments, hearts at ease.

In shadows where secrets dwell,
Breaths entwined with dreams we chase.
Echoes weave a timeless spell,
Filling the empty space.

With each heartbeat, we will find,
Fragments of a lost refrain.
Curved echoes of the mind,
Remind us where we've been, again.

So let us dance within this flow,
As stars flicker in the night.
Curved echoes, soft and slow,
Guide us to the morning light.

The Maze of Longing

In a labyrinth of the heart,
Each turn holds a hidden sigh.
Paths entwined, we drift apart,
Yet the flame refuses to die.

Wandering through tangled dreams,
Every corner feels so near.
Faint echoes of our schemes,
Whisper wishes, bittersweet dear.

Lost in echoes of the past,
Labyrinthine hopes remain.
Every shadow holds a cast,
Longing etched in joy and pain.

With every step, the walls confine,
Yet still, I'm drawn to your light.
In this maze, your heart is mine,
Guiding me through endless night.

Though the winding paths confuse,
In the center, I will stand.
In this maze, I choose to lose,
For in longing, love's the hand.

Spirals of Reflection

In still waters of the mind,
Ripples dance like fleeting thoughts.
Each spiral, a truth to find,
In silence, battles are fought.

We spiral down through the years,
Memories whisper and twine.
Joy entwined with shadowed fears,
Life's a delicate design.

Mirrors show the tales we weave,
Layers deep with vibrant hue.
In this depth, we learn to believe,
Spirals reflect what's true.

An endless journey within,
Thoughts collide and worlds collide.
Each reflection, a new skin,
Embracing all that we hide.

Through spirals, our spirits soar,
Finding beauty in the strife.
In reflection, we restore,
Embracing the dance of life.

The Forgotten Corners

In forgotten corners, we roam,
Dusty memories linger on.
Each shadow feels like a home,
In the echoes of the dawn.

Whispers trapped in vaulted space,
Threads of laughter intertwined.
Time has worn a gentle face,
In the silence, hearts align.

Cobwebs cradle tales untold,
Photographs begin to fade.
Stories woven, bright and bold,
In these corners, love parade.

Windows cracked let in the light,
Illuminating faded dreams.
Searching for what feels so right,
In forgotten corners, gleams.

So let us wander, hand in hand,
Through the memories that remain.
In these corners, we will stand,
Finding joy in loss and gain.

Journeys Within

In shadows deep where secrets lie,
The heart embarks, the spirit flies.
A silent call, the whispers start,
To venture forth and find the heart.

Narrow paths of thought unwind,
In quiet moments, truth we find.
The road is long, the pace is slow,
Yet every step, the self will grow.

Through tangled dreams and fleeting fears,
We travel on, beyond the years.
Each twist and turn, a tale unfolds,
In journeys where the mind beholds.

The echoes of the past will guide,
Through inner realms, we will decide.
Amidst the chaos, find the calm,
Within ourselves, we draft a psalm.

In the end, the light we seek,
Is found in silence, not in speak.
The journey's worth, the lessons learned,
In sacred space, our hearts are turned.

Fractured Mirrors

Shards of glass reflect the soul,
Broken pieces, yet feel whole.
Each crack reveals a different view,
A fractured truth, but still so true.

Glimmers dance in scattered rays,
Echoes of forgotten days.
In every shard, a story told,
Of dreams once bright, now tinged with gold.

The beauty in the flawed we find,
In every edge, a depth of mind.
We learn to love what's torn apart,
For in the cracks lies hidden art.

So let us gather all the shards,
And piece them back, disregarding guards.
For in the merging of our tales,
A stronger self within prevails.

In mirrors broke, reflections shine,
A mosaic of the heart divine.
Embrace the imperfections here,
In every fault, the truth is clear.

Depths of Introspection

In silent waters, thoughts cascade,
A realm where hopes and fears invade.
Beneath the surface, shadows play,
In depths where light begins to sway.

Here dreams are woven with the night,
Reflections masked in soft twilight.
In introspection, truths reside,
Through every wave, we turn the tide.

As currents pull, we dive and sink,
Exploring depths, we pause to think.
What lies below, what waits to see,
Uncovered layers of you and me.

Each ripple holds a whispered voice,
In solitude, we learn to choice.
To face the dark, embrace the light,
In depths of self, we find our sight.

To journey inward, brave the storms,
Through shadowed paths, we shape new forms.
In depths where silence finds its grace,
We cherish every sacred space.

Labyrinthine Whispers

Winding paths of thought entwine,
In every corner, secrets shine.
A maze of dreams, both wide and tight,
Where whispers dance in fleeting light.

Each turn reveals a brand new way,
A tapestry of night and day.
Threads woven with intention clear,
Guide us through what we hold dear.

In silence speaks the heart's desire,
Through tangled trails, we rise, aspire.
In labyrinths of mind and time,
The journey weaves a perfect rhyme.

The echoes of the past resound,
In every breath, a truth is found.
Through winding ways our spirits roam,
In whispers soft, we find our home.

With every step, a chance to grow,
In labyrinthine light, we flow.
To navigate the twists we face,
And honor every sacred place.

Dimensions of Self

In shadows deep, I search within,
Layers unfold, a dance of kin.
A mirror shows, both light and shade,
The self, a puzzle yet displayed.

Voices call from times gone by,
Echoes of laughter, a silent cry.
With every step, I seek and find,
New facets of this heart and mind.

A warrior dreams, a lover weeps,
In every thread, the soul it keeps.
With open hands, I grasp the air,
Embrace the journey, shed despair.

Through every trial, I rise anew,
With whispered hopes, I dare pursue.
In every form, my spirit's grace,
A boundless realm, a sacred space.

In dimensions vast, I make my stand,
A tapestry drawn by fate's own hand.
Through storms and calm, I learn to see,
The myriad selves that dance in me.

The Mind's Minotaur

In labyrinths where thoughts collide,
I chase the shadows, nowhere to hide.
A beast of fear, it prowls within,
In tangled paths where doubts begin.

With every twist, I face the truth,
Fleeting moments of fleeting youth.
The corridors echo with my cries,
In maze-like binds, the spirit flies.

A flicker of hope in darkest night,
Guides me forth with fragile light.
To confront the beast, I must be brave,
In this arena, I shall not cave.

Each step I take, the air grows thin,
A dance with shadows, where fears begin.
Yet through the dark, the heart will soar,
Unlocking doors, forever more.

I wield my courage, a beacon's flare,
The Minotaur trembles, met with despair.
In this wild maze, I'll find my song,
For in my truth, I will belong.

Hidden Corners of Being

In hidden nooks where silence dwells,
Whispers of secrets, time retells.
Unseen wonders, the heart's delight,
In quiet moments, shadows ignite.

The gentle breeze where dreams confide,
Nurturing thoughts that cannot hide.
In corners soft, the soul can breathe,
With every sigh, the world weaves.

A tapestry of hopes and fears,
In hidden places, laughter cheers.
A sanctuary, where I can grow,
In the stillness, wisdom flows.

Found in the cracks of life's design,
A sacred space, a treasure mine.
In shadows deep, I find my spark,
Illuminating paths once dark.

Through hidden corners, life reveals,
The quiet power that healing heals.
With open eyes, the heart takes flight,
In every being, shines the light.

Veiled Pathways to Truth

In veiled pathways, truth resides,
Masked in silence, where wisdom hides.
Through layers thick, the heart will yearn,
For light to pierce, for fires to burn.

A journey steeped in questions deep,
Awakening dreams from slumber's keep.
Each step I take, the fog will clear,
To uncover what I hold dear.

With courage bold, I walk the line,
Between the known and the divine.
In every sorrow, a seed is sown,
Truth grows strong, its roots have grown.

A compass forged from love and pain,
Guides me through the falling rain.
Searching the depths, I start to see,
Veils that shroud humanity.

Through veiled pathways, my heart takes flight,
In every shadow, a spark of light.
To grasp the truth, I must be brave,
Within these paths, my soul I save.

Embracing the Unknown

In the stillness of the night,
Whispers call from the dark,
Step forth into the void,
With courage as your spark.

Dreams unfold like petals,
Revealing hidden views,
With each stride into the mist,
New horizons to choose.

Fear not the shadowed trails,
For light will find its way,
Embrace the silent realms,
Where possibilities sway.

With every choice unfurling,
The path will start to glow,
Trust in the steps you take,
In the unknown, you grow.

The heart beats a soft rhythm,
A compass in the night,
Follow its gentle whispers,
And dance in pure delight.

Fragments of Lost Memories

Tattered photographs linger,
Dust clings to the years,
Echoes of laughter float,
Carried by unseen tears.

Faded scents of childhood,
Colors dimmed with time,
Each fragment holds a secret,
Wrapped in a gentle rhyme.

Worn out shoes on the porch,
Stories carved in wood,
Whispers of distant moments,
Remembering all that stood.

In shadows of the past,
Time weaves its tender thread,
Connecting hearts and souls,
To the love that's never dead.

To hold these precious pieces,
Is to cherish what is lost,
A tapestry of memory,
With beauty at its cost.

Passageways of the Heart

Through winding trails of feeling,
We wander hand in hand,
Each twist a new discovery,
In a vast and tender land.

Words spoken in soft whispers,
Bridge the depths we see,
Binding souls with gentle threads,
Creating harmony.

Moments wrapped in silence,
Yet deeply understood,
In the echo of our laughter,
We find our sacred good.

Each heartbeat paints a pathway,
Each glance ignites a flame,
The passageways of the heart,
Where love can know no name.

In this dance of souls entwined,
We're free to be our own,
Through the corridors of trust,
In love, we have grown.

Unseen Pathways

Beneath the fog of morning,
Lie journeys yet to tread,
With every step we wander,
Unseen paths lie ahead.

Nature speaks in riddles,
Whispers flow through the air,
Each rustling leaf a promise,
That adventure waits somewhere.

Through forests thick with wonder,
Through fields of wild embrace,
The heart beats ever onward,
In search of a sacred place.

Footprints may fade away,
But the spirit remains clear,
Guiding us through spaces,
Where dreams dare not to fear.

Let the unknown beckon softly,
With hope as our trusted light,
For unseen pathways lead us,
Into the arms of the night.

The Dark Corners of Reflection

In shadows deep, where whispers dwell,
The echoes of my fears do swell.
Each thought a ghost that haunts the night,
In silence wrapped, I search for light.

Mirrors crack with secrets old,
Silhouettes of stories told.
I wander through this twilight maze,
Chasing dawn through misty haze.

Behind closed doors, regrets reside,
With every glance, a fleeting tide.
Yet hope remains a flick'ring flame,
To guide me on despite the shame.

Reflections craft a fragile art,
Each shard a piece of broken heart.
In darkened corners, truth is found,
A lesson learned, profound, unbound.

Nebula of Thoughts

In swirling dust of cosmic light,
My mind ignites the endless night.
Galaxies spin with dreams yet born,
Each star a wish, from heart to scorn.

Nebulas dance in purple glow,
Thoughts collide, both fast and slow.
A tapestry of wild designs,
Where chaos brews and fate intertwines.

Fragments float, like whispers shared,
Ideas clash, but none are spared.
Through meteor fields, I steer my way,
Seeking clarity in disarray.

Cosmic winds take me afar,
Where wonders thrive among the stars.
In silence, wisdom starts to bloom,
A universe concealed in gloom.

Through the Veiled Corridor

A corridor of whispers calls,
Where light and shadow gently falls.
Each step I take, a veil I part,
Unearthing truths within the heart.

Walls adorned with tales untold,
Ink and memories seep like gold.
Images flicker, lost in time,
Echoes of life, in prose and rhyme.

As I walk through this quiet space,
I find the courage to embrace.
What lies behind the curtain's sway,
Is freedom's kiss at break of day.

Veils of doubt may drape the way,
Yet hope persists—a brighter day.
Through corridors both wide and small,
I learn that love can conquer all.

Paths of Uncertainty

In shadows cast by doubt's embrace,
I tread the paths with caution, grace.
Each step uncertain, whispers flee,
Yet every road unveils the sea.

A fork appears, decisions weigh,
Which route to take, come what may?
With every choice, a lesson grows,
In tangled woods, the heart bestows.

Winding trails that lead to fate,
Through valleys wide, I contemplate.
The pulse of life, a rhythmic dance,
In moments fleeting, find romance.

Though fog may shroud the course ahead,
I follow signs that hope has bled.
Each path a story yet to weave,
In uncertainty, I dare believe.

Secrets of the Inner Chamber

In shadows deep where voices fade,
A heart concealed beneath the shade.
Whispers dance, in silence they play,
Unlock the door, let truth hold sway.

Dreams entwined in a secret thread,
Echoes linger of words unsaid.
Hidden places where hopes reside,
Amidst the corners, love and pride.

Each glance a promise, each breath a sigh,
Guarded treasures, oh, how they lie.
In the stillness, the mysteries bloom,
Filling the emptiness of the room.

Fragments lost in time's embrace,
Stories woven in silent grace.
Unraveled tales, the heart expands,
In the chamber of forgotten sands.

One last secret, softly revealed,
The most cherished, now unsealed.
Let echoes guide with gentle call,
To the chamber where dreams enthrall.

A Tapestry of Whispers

Threads of silence, woven tight,
In the fabric of the night.
Whispers travel, soft and low,
A tapestry of tales to flow.

Intricate patterns, secrets spun,
Stories hidden, slowly begun.
Colors bright and shadows deep,
In this weave, their promises seep.

Each strand a voice, each hue a thought,
In the loom of time, they're gently caught.
From heart to heart, the whispers travel,
Unraveling truths, as they unravel.

In the quiet, listen close,
To the murmur of shadows, it knows.
As dawn approaches, they blend as one,
A whispered dream beneath the sun.

A touch of grace in every seam,
We are stitched together, a shared dream.
In the tapestry of life we weave,
Connected souls, forever believe.

Gates of Perception

A gateway stands, beckoning wide,
To worlds unseen, where shadows hide.
Beyond the threshold, truth and lies,
In colors bright, unseen skies.

Through the lattice of time, we peep,
Past the mundane, where secrets seep.
An echo calls, a voice so clear,
Pulling hearts and dreams near.

What lies within, a weightless haze,
In riddles spoken, lost in a maze.
Every door a chance to flee,
Or discover the depths of we.

Far-flung realms, the mind expands,
In vaulted whispers, hope commands.
Yet caution lingers, shadows play,
At the gates where visions sway.

In the balance of light and dark,
Perception shifts, igniting a spark.
Step forth, brave soul, embrace the quest,
At the gates of thought, you'll find your rest.

Maps of the Unseen

Drawn in ink, lines of the past,
Maps of the unseen, shadows cast.
Navigate dreams, where hearts combine,
In the depths of the vast design.

Lost in folds of time's embrace,
Each wrinkle tells a hidden place.
On paper dreams take flight and soar,
To realms where souls seek evermore.

Markers etched in whispered tones,
Pulse of the earth, the language of stones.
Journey forth, through night and day,
To the hidden paths that light the way.

In this map, the unknown gleams,
A tapestry of drifting dreams.
Follow the lines, let instincts steer,
Maps of the unseen, ever near.

To wander, to wonder, open your eyes,
In each step lies a sweet surprise.
Embrace the journey, heart's decree,
In maps of the unseen, you will be free.

Shadows of Self-Discovery

In the quiet, whispers grow,
Lost in realms we seldom know.
Silent echoes call our name,
Flickering flames, igniting flame.

Footsteps trace the paths we've sown,
Through dark woods, we walk alone.
Shadows dance, revealing light,
In our depths, we find the fight.

Mirrored thoughts, a fractured maze,
In the night, our spirits blaze.
Every turn a brand-new chance,
Through the shadows, we advance.

With each step, we shed our guise,
Face the truth, unveil the lies.
In the silence, wisdom sings,
Opening doors to hidden wings.

Within these shadows, we transform,
Embrace the dark, ignite the storm.
Journey deep, let courage swell,
In the shadows, we find ourselves.

Mirrors of the Heart

Reflections dance in pools of dreams,
Whispers soft as silver beams.
Each glance reveals a hidden part,
Layered truths within the heart.

In every gaze, a story told,
Love unfolds as time grows bold.
Fragments shine, like scattered stars,
Braiding light where shadow spars.

Feelings linger, bittersweet,
In our depths, the echoes meet.
Mirrors show what we may hide,
Within their depths, we can't divide.

Each heartbeat syncs with fate's design,
Seeing self where worlds entwine.
In the glass, we find our way,
Guided through the night and day.

In these mirrors, love's embrace,
Time reveals the truest face.
Through each tear, a gentle art,
Reflecting back the beating heart.

Secrets Beneath the Surface

Whispers echo in the stream,
Life's mysteries, a hidden dream.
Beneath the waves, the silence grows,
In the depths, the secret flows.

Veils of water, shifting light,
Revealing truths in shadowed sight.
Underneath, the currents pull,
Lessons learned, a heart so full.

In the stillness, secrets stir,
Nature's heartbeat, soft as fur.
Every ripple tells a tale,
Of silent winds and sails that fail.

Beneath the surface, life unfolds,
Hidden gems and stories bold.
Time will show what's long concealed,
In the depths, we are revealed.

Secrets whispered through the years,
Flowing gently, calming fears.
In the water's gentle sway,
We find peace in yesterday.

Twists of Thought

In the maze of winding paths,
Thoughts collide, embrace the wrath.
Ideas spin like autumn leaves,
Dancing wild, no one believes.

Every twist a fresh surprise,
Unraveling truth in disguise.
Chasing shadows, we take flight,
Journeying deep into the night.

Questions rise like morning mist,
Challenging the heart's soft twist.
Mind's playground, a vivid scene,
Finding solace in between.

In the labyrinth of our dreams,
Possibilities burst at the seams.
Every turn, a lesson learned,
Through the chaos, wisdom churned.

From these thoughts, we weave our tale,
Navigating through each gale.
In the twists, we come to know,
The beauty in the endless flow.

Enigmas of the Soul

In shadows deep, the whispers call,
Secrets hidden, unseen to all.
A flicker of truth, a glint of light,
Lost in the depth of endless night.

Echoes of laughter, a fleeting sigh,
Chasing reflections that dance and fly.
In labyrinths formed by wish and dream,
The soul's raw canvas, a silent scream.

Threads of hope woven tight in the fray,
Lost in the maze where fears hold sway.
Yet courage blooms where shadows persist,
Embracing the path, the heart's gentle twist.

Unravel the layers, peel back the skin,
Find solace within, where shadows begin.
An endless journey, a quest unknown,
In every corner, a truth is sown.

Through the enigmas, we rise and fall,
In the silent chambers, we hear the call.
Each riddle faced, our spirit blooms,
A tapestry woven from mystic rooms.

Fragmented Realities

Shattered mirrors reflecting dreams,
Lost in the silence, unraveling seams.
A world divided by choices made,
Fragments of truths in twilight shade.

Lost in the echo of voices past,
In myriad paths, shadows are cast.
Moments collide, a dance so bold,
Stories waiting to be retold.

A tapestry woven from threads so fine,
Each fragment whispering, no clear line.
Colors bleeding, within the gray,
The heart seeks solace in disarray.

Amidst the chaos, clarity gleams,
From shattered pieces, new vision beams.
Through veils of doubt, the light will break,
In fragmented worlds, a bond we make.

Reality bends, yet truth holds tight,
Guiding our steps through the haunting night.
Each fragment a lesson, a piece of the whole,
Within the chaos, we find the soul.

The Maze of Memories

Winding paths in a fleeting mind,
Lost in the echoes of what we find.
Dusty corridors hold tales untold,
In the maze of memories, the heart is bold.

Familiar faces flicker and fade,
Moments of laughter, the warmth of aid.
A labyrinth formed of joy and pain,
In the winding twists, both sunshine and rain.

Each turn reveals a story anew,
Forgotten whispers, a haunting view.
Fragments of bliss, shadows of dread,
In the maze of memories, our hearts are led.

Through alleys of laughter, through valleys of tears,
We navigate time, confronting our fears.
Holding tight to the light that remains,
As we walk through the maze, our essence sustains.

Guided by echoes of who we were,
The maze will shift, yet we will endure.
In the labyrinth's heart, we seek the thread,
Connecting the moments that lie ahead.

Spirals of Insight

Round and round, the thoughts will spin,
Seeking the wisdom that dwells within.
A spiral of questions, tangled and bright,
In the dance of the mind, we find our light.

Layers unfolding like petals in bloom,
Unraveling secrets, dispelling the gloom.
With each turn taken, the vision grows clear,
The spiral whispers what we long to hear.

Through twists of fate, we gather our learn,
In the fire of insights, our spirits discern.
A dance of the heart, entwined with the soul,
In spirals of wisdom, we find our role.

The journey winds on, no end in sight,
Each insight gained, a flicker of light.
In the arms of the spiral, we glide and sway,
Embracing the path, come what may.

For within the spirals, revelations sing,
Echoing softly, a beautiful thing.
In the heart of the spiral, we find our grace,
In endless journeys, we find our place.

Passageways of the Spirit

Through whispered winds, we find our way,
In silent corridors where shadows play.
Echoes of truth in every breath,
Guiding us softly, beyond life and death.

The heartbeat of night, a soft refrain,
A tapestry woven with joy and pain.
We wander through dreams, our souls aflame,
In the passageways, we lose and reclaim.

Mysteries linger, wrapped in the dark,
With every step, we ignite the spark.
Illuminated paths, gentle and wide,
Inviting the spirit to dance and glide.

The light of the dawn beckons us near,
A whisper of hope that banishes fear.
Each doorway we open reveals the more,
A journey of love that we can't ignore.

In the tapestry of time, we weave our string,
Finding our voices in the songs we sing.
Passageways beckon, souls intertwine,
Creating a symphony, sacred and divine.

Entrances to the Within

In the stillness of night, a door creaks wide,
Leading us inward, where secrets abide.
Each entrance whispers of tales untold,
Of fears and fables, of brave and bold.

Windows of thought, in reflections we find,
The echo of dreams, the threads that bind.
We venture inside, where the heart beats slow,
Unraveling shadows, watching them grow.

Gates made of silence, walls steeped in lore,
Within every crack, a mystic's score.
Unlocking the library of what we are,
Glimpses of wisdom, shining like stars.

Winding corridors of the soul's design,
Paths of emotion, both yours and mine.
Entrances invite us, each one a path,
Leading us deeper, igniting our wrath.

As we seek the depths, our spirits will soar,
Finding our truth in the depths of the core.
Entrances to within, to the vast unknown,
Discovering more, embracing the grown.

The Mapless Journey

With no maps to guide us, we venture forth,
Into the embrace of the unseen worth.
Stars overhead, our only light,
As we wander through the endless night.

Each step is a dance, each moment a chance,
Finding our rhythm in the cosmic dance.
Winding the roads with hearts unconfined,
Lost in the beauty of space and time.

The destination elusive, yet close to our heart,
We learn to let go, to play our part.
In the journey, we find what we seek,
Strength in the silence, solace in the meek.

With winds as our compass, and dreams as our guide,
We wander the shores with the moon as our pride.
The mapless journey, a canvas unfurled,
Crafting our stories, painting the world.

As we travel this path, we discover the weave,
Of everything felt, and all we believe.
In the moments we share, through love and despair,
The mapless journey unfolds everywhere.

Shadows of the Unsaid

In whispers of twilight, truths linger near,
Bathed in the silence, we hold our fear.
Words left unspoken, trapped in the air,
Creating the shadows, we cannot share.

Beneath every glance, a universe spins,
The weight of the heart where longing begins.
Shadows that echo the things we conceal,
In the depths of our souls, they silently kneel.

Each moment a canvas, painted with doubt,
What's left unexpressed, we quietly shout.
Within the silence, the stories reside,
In the shadows of unsaid, our truths divide.

Echoes of laughter, a ghost in the light,
What we never voiced still colors the night.
Shadows will wander, haunting the mind,
Searching for solace, that we cannot find.

So let us break free, let the words take flight,
To unveil the shadows, to ignite the light.
In the echoes of heartbeats, our voices rise,
Shadows of the unsaid, become our skies.

Portraits of Solitude

In quiet corners where shadows play,
Whispers linger in hues of gray.
Moments stretch like the afternoon light,
Each heartbeat echoes, a soft, faint fight.

Ghostly echoes of laughter roam,
Secluded realms, an unwritten tome.
The breath of solitude stirs the air,
A tranquil pulse, a thought laid bare.

Beneath the stars, a silence profound,
The mind's confessions in darkness found.
Every sigh, a story untold,
Wrapped in dreams, both tender and bold.

In the stillness, shadows dance,
Each lingering thought finds its chance.
Loneliness wears a fragile crown,
In its embrace, I willingly drown.

Through the window, the world moves fast,
But in this moment, I breathe the past.
Each breath a canvas, painted anew,
Portraits of solitude, vibrant and true.

The Enchanted Mindscape

In a realm where visions take flight,
Dreams intertwine with the depth of night.
Colors swirl like a river of time,
Painting whispers in soft, sweet rhyme.

Thoughts unfurl like petals in bloom,
Each one a spark dispelling the gloom.
Imagination, a canvas so wide,
A place where secrets and wonders abide.

Starlit paths beckon from afar,
Guiding the heart where the wild things are.
Echoes of laughter ripple like waves,
In the enchanted mindscape, adventure braves.

Lost in the mazes of magical lore,
Visions converge as they flow and soar.
Each fleeting moment, a treasure, a gem,
In this tapestry, I lose my hem.

With every heartbeat, the story unfolds,
In colors vibrant, the silence holds.
A journey of thought, a blissful flight,
In this enchanted mindscape, bathed in light.

Gossamer Pathways

Through the forest of wandering streams,
Gossamer pathways weave through dreams.
Sunlight filters soft through the trees,
A symphony whispered by the breeze.

Footsteps dance on a carpet of leaves,
Nature's embrace, a heart that believes.
Each turn reveals a secret or two,
Where magic mingles in shades of blue.

Cascading laughter of water flows,
Guiding the soul where the wildflower grows.
With every step, a promise made,
On gossamer pathways, fears start to fade.

Clouds drift softly in skies so vast,
Memories linger, entwined with the past.
In every corner, a tale to tell,
Gossamer pathways, where wonders dwell.

The sun sets low, painting skies afire,
As twilight lingers, stoking desire.
Each journey carved in soft, gentle sighs,
On gossamer pathways, the spirit flies.

Reflections in Labyrinths

In shadows deep where echoes collide,
Labyrinths stretch with secrets inside.
Mirrored whispers beckon my gaze,
A dance of thoughts in a winding maze.

At each corner, the past unwinds,
Drawing memories from the hidden binds.
Reflections shimmer on crisp, calm pools,
In these labyrinths, we find our rules.

Flickering flames of forgotten dreams,
Illuminate pathways in silvery beams.
Each step I take, a story reborn,
In the heart of the maze, a silence worn.

Fragments of time in swirling mist,
Labyrinths wrap us in fate's soft twist.
Every choice a thread of fate,
Leading us closer, or suggesting wait.

Within these walls, truth dances bold,
In reflections of the past, we are told.
Winding deeper into the unknown,
Reflections in labyrinths, where we have grown.

Whispers of the Soul's Maze

In the corners where shadows play,
Silent whispers softly sway.
Echoes of secrets chase the light,
Guiding hearts through the night.

Hidden paths of gentle sighs,
Where the truth in silence lies.
Footsteps dance on dreams untold,
In the maze, the brave and bold.

Each turn reveals a buried thought,
In the stillness, battles fought.
Winding roads, the heart's embrace,
In this sanctuary, find your place.

Threads of hope in shadows spun,
Tracing the paths where love begun.
With every choice, a choice displaced,
In the maze, time's softest grace.

Whispers linger, fading slow,
In the depths, we come to know.
The soul's maze, a tapestry,
Woven with threads of mystery.

Echoes in the Mind's Hallway

Footsteps echo down the lane,
Memories pulse like gentle rain.
In the stillness, voices call,
Resonating through the hall.

Fragments of laughter drift near,
Whispers of joy, tinged with fear.
In each corner, shadows play,
Guiding thoughts that fade away.

Walls adorned with dreams once bright,
Flicker like stars in the night.
Each turn reveals a silent plea,
Yearning for what used to be.

And if you listen with your heart,
You'll find the echoes never part.
In the mind's vast, winding ways,
Memory's dance forever stays.

Traces linger, soft and clear,
Carrying whispers held so dear.
In the hallway of our mind,
The past and present intertwine.

Veils of Reflection

In the stillness where waters gleam,
Lie the veils that weave a dream.
Gentle ripples tell the tale,
Of hearts that hope and sometimes fail.

Each reflection whispers low,
Stories of love and loss we know.
Rippling echoes softly blend,
In this realm where visions mend.

Veils of truth, so thin yet strong,
Reveal the places we belong.
With every glance, a deeper dive,
In the depths, we come alive.

Glimmers of a brighter day,
Woven in the shadows' play.
Beneath the surface, dreams do swell,
In reflective waters, all is well.

Find your essence in this pool,
Let the veils of doubt become the tool.
To uncover worlds anew,
In reflections, find your view.

Paths Winding Within

Winding paths beneath the skin,
Lead to places held within.
Each decision, every choice,
In the chambers, hear your voice.

Through the labyrinth of the mind,
Secrets of the soul unwind.
In the quiet, shadows play,
Guiding our dreams day by day.

Every fork holds tales untold,
Paths of silver, paths of gold.
Follow where your heart does steer,
In the whispers, find what's dear.

Journey through the winding ways,
In the puzzle, there's always grace.
Footsteps merge with time's embrace,
Inward paths, a sacred space.

At each turn, embrace the spin,
For every loss, there's something to win.
Winding paths, both dark and bright,
Guide the traveler toward the light.

Refracted Thoughts

In shadows cast by fleeting light,
Ideas twist, like dreams in flight.
Each glimmer hides a tale untold,
In fractured beams, our minds unfold.

We chase reflections, bright and dim,
Unraveling paths, both near and him.
Through prisms' dance, our thoughts entwine,
In every color, truth will shine.

We ponder deep, lost in delight,
Searching for clarity in the night.
With every turn, new facets gleam,
Awakening the dormant dream.

Yet, in confusion's hazy veil,
We find our voices, soft but frail.
Through refracted echoes, hope is found,
In the silence, we're spellbound.

So let us wander, stripped of fear,
In the light of thoughts, crystal clear.
For every fracture tells a story,
In refracted paths, we find our glory.

Mysterious Labors of the Heart

In silent chambers, secrets dwell,
Whispers echo, spells they tell.
Fingers trace the depths of soul,
In shadowed corners, we are whole.

With every beat, a question grows,
What lies beneath this heart that knows?
Tangled threads of fear and grace,
In labyrinths, our dreams we chase.

The heart laboring, day by day,
Navigating love's intricate play.
A canvas painted with the past,
Each stroke a memory, unsurpassed.

Time weaves its tapestry bright,
Twisting paths of wrong and right.
Yet through the struggle, we shall find,
The ties that bind are love defined.

In the stillness, truths appear,
Mysterious labors, tender, dear.
With every pulse, we gather strength,
In the heart's labor, we find length.

Beneath the Surface Waves

Upon the crest, the ocean sighs,
A restless dance beneath the skies.
Beneath the waves, a world concealed,
Where whispered tales are long revealed.

Curious depths of azure blue,
Harboring dreams both old and new.
In tangled seaweed, life takes form,
In gentle currents, hearts keep warm.

The waves, they rise, their stories clash,
In salty breezes, echoes splash.
Yet underneath, a calm resides,
As mysteries flow with changing tides.

To dive below, where silence reigns,
In tranquil depths, the spirit gains.
Embracing currents, fears we sever,
In the abyss, we find forever.

So let us plunge, break through the lace,
Beneath the surface, find our place.
In waves of thought, we drift and sway,
To the silent calls of the deep array.

Caves of the Self

In caves of the self, echoes breathe,
Stories whispered from below heave.
Chiseled from shadows, our truths arise,
In darkness, we search for the skies.

Stalactites hang like dreams deferred,
Each drip a memory, softly stirred.
Through caverns deep, the heart explores,
Seeking light behind the hidden doors.

Walls lined with fears, yet still we climb,
In silence, we find the rhythm of time.
Each twist and turn reveals a spark,
Illuminating the hidden dark.

Resilience whispers within the stone,
In caves of the self, we are never alone.
We gather strength from echoes around,
In the secret chambers, we're profoundly found.

So venture forth into the unknown,
For in these caves, our truth is sown.
With every step, a tale unfolds,
In the caves of the self, our spirit molds.

The Echoing Silence

In a room where whispers fade,
Soft shadows dance in light's parade.
The walls hold secrets, deep and wide,
In echo's grasp, we must abide.

Lost in thoughts that twist and roam,
Fleeting moments of a home.
Time stands still, yet moves so swift,
In silence here, our dreams uplift.

The ticking clock, a haunting beats,
In stillness, soul and silence meet.
With every breath, the quiet sighs,
Beneath the calm, a storm still lies.

Outside the world, a vibrant hue,
While here we sit, just me and you.
In echo's hold, we find our space,
A tranquil pause, a warm embrace.

Yet silence speaks in whispered tones,
Of love and loss, of fading moans.
In echoes clear, the truths align,
A world of silence, yet divine.

Forks Beneath the Skin

Beneath the surface, choices hide,
Paths entwined, nowhere to bide.
Forks of fate that shift and sway,
In shadows deep, we lose our way.

Each mark upon the skin does tell,
Of battles fought, of heaven and hell.
Stories woven in each line,
In every scar, a tale divine.

Yet still we wander, heart in hand,
Searching for a promised land.
In every fork, a chance to grow,
A chance to learn, a chance to know.

The mirrors reflect our chosen turns,
With every glance, a fire burns.
In skin so tender, dreams are sown,
A map of who we've always known.

And so we stand at every gate,
Decisions lined; it's never late.
With courage found, we brave the night,
For forks beneath the skin bring light.

Labyrinthine Dreams

In corridors of twilight's gleam,
Wanderers lost in tangled dreams.
Paths obscure, with whispers low,
Where shadows stretch and time moves slow.

Each turn a choice, a door to fate,
With hearts uncertain, we navigate.
The walls are etched with hopes and fears,
Reflecting joy and stifled tears.

Golden threads of light arise,
Guiding souls through maze-like ties.
In dreams, we dance, we fight, we fall,
Seeking answers in the call.

Yet in this labyrinth, we find grace,
With every twist, a warm embrace.
A haven where our spirits soar,
In boundless dreams forevermore.

Through winding paths, we grasp the truth,
Of age-old wisdom, lost in youth.
In labyrinthine dreams, we yearn,
To find the light and brightly burn.

Chasing the Lost Echo

In valleys deep where shadows lay,
We chase the sound, the echo's play.
A fleeting voice that calls us near,
A whisper lost, yet crystal clear.

Through forests thick with silent trees,
We follow hopes upon the breeze.
Each step we take, the past awakes,
In echoes rich, the heart partakes.

The mountains loom, they guard our quest,
With every heartbeat, we are blessed.
In every turn, a memory stirs,
In rhythm soft, the longing purrs.

Yet echoes fade like breath in air,
We chase the lost, yet find despair.
But in the chase, there lies the spark,
In seeking light, we leave our mark.

So journey on, and don't relent,
For echoes sung are heaven-sent.
In every chase, new echoes rise,
To guide our hearts toward the skies.

Vistas Within

In shadows deep, the soul does roam,
Exploring vistas far from home.
Each whisper soft, a secret shared,
Unveiling dreams, the heart has dared.

In twilight's glow, the visions play,
With colors bright, they melt away.
A garden rich with memory's seed,
Each bloom a tale, each thorn a need.

The quiet mind, a canvas wide,
Where thoughts align, where fears abide.
In silence found, the truth will shine,
Eclipsing doubt, divine design.

Through winding paths of hopes and sighs,
We search for light in endless skies.
With every step, a piece of grace,
Emerging from the hidden space.

Vistas within, yet to behold,
Each heartbeat sings, each breath is told.
In life's embrace, we come alive,
Inward journey, the soul will thrive.

Riddles of the Heart

In shadows cast where whispers dwell,
The heart's confessions weave a spell.
With every pulse, a question grows,
Unraveling what no one knows.

In tangled thoughts, emotions twist,
A haunting melody persists.
Each smile a mask, each tear a clue,
In riddles spoken, love shines through.

Beneath the stars, desires ignite,
In sleepless nights, we chase the light.
What truths emerge when souls entwine?
What lies beneath the heart's design?

With every laugh, a story told,
In glances shared, the mysteries unfold.
A labyrinth wide, where passions start,
Exploring deep the riddles of the heart.

The silence speaks in gentle prose,
In whispered dreams, the longing grows.
For in the chaos, love's refrain,
Is found in loss, in joy's domain.

Unraveling Threads

In twilight's edge, the fabric frays,
As life unfurls in tangled ways.
Each thread a story, woven tight,
In shades of dark, in hues of light.

With gentle hands, we weave and mend,
In every knot, a chance to bend.
Through trials faced, through time entwined,
Unraveling threads, the heart aligned.

A tapestry rich, of love and pain,
In patterns formed, in joy and rain.
Each stitch a moment, stitched with care,
In every fabric, memories share.

Through seasons change, the colors shift,
In shadows cast, the spirits lift.
With grace we find, amidst the dread,
A wiser heart from threads we've shed.

The loom of life, it weaves and spins,
Creating warmth where hope begins.
In every heart, a story kernel,
Unraveling threads, the gift eternal.

Footsteps in the Mind's Garden

In stillness brought by evening's grace,
Footsteps echo in the quiet space.
The mind's own garden, lush and wide,
With blooms of thought where dreams abide.

Through winding paths that lead away,
We gather seeds from yesterday.
In fragrant air, ideas sprout,
In whispered thoughts, we roam about.

The petals soft, the thorns they teach,
Of lessons learned, of goals to reach.
With every step, a chance to grow,
In the heart's garden, dreams will flow.

Beneath the stars, the shadows dance,
In the twilight glow, we take our chance.
With every heartbeat, life is penned,
In footsteps taken, our tales extend.

In the mind's embrace, where wonders dwell,
We wander on, the stories swell.
With open hearts, our paths align,
In the garden, dreams intertwine.

Whispers of the Heart

In the quiet moments, we find our truth,
Soft echoes linger, a gentle proof.
Words unspoken weave through the air,
Whispers of love, beyond compare.

Stars dance softly in the night,
Guiding our souls with pure delight.
In every heartbeat, a story hides,
Whispers of hope, where time abides.

Embers flicker in the dark,
Kindling flames with a single spark.
Drawn together by fate's sweet art,
Unlocking the whispers of the heart.

Memories linger, like a soft sigh,
Carried on breezes, they drift by.
In the stillness, a promise awaits,
Whispers of dreams that love creates.

Through the shadows, we shall roam,
Finding our way, we are never alone.
Let the whispers guide us, steady and clear,
Whispers of the heart, forever near.

Threads of Consciousness

In the tapestry of thought, we weave,
Bright threads of essence that we believe.
Each idea dances on the loom,
Threads of consciousness, a silent bloom.

Golden moments glisten and fade,
Captured in shadows that time made.
We stroll through dreams, both vivid and stark,
Threads connect us, igniting a spark.

In the web of wonder, the mind's delight,
Ideas swirling, taking flight.
A gentle pull, a guiding hand,
Threads of consciousness, a vast expanse.

Questions linger like echoes in night,
Searching for answers wrapped in light.
Every thought a thread we share,
Woven together with love and care.

As the dawn breaks, we rise and see,
The threads intertwining, setting us free.
In the fabric of life, our stories blend,
Threads of consciousness that never end.

Secrets Beneath the Surface

Beneath the calm, the currents glide,
Secrets whisper, where shadows hide.
Silent stories call from the deep,
Secrets beneath the surface keep.

Echoes of laughter, echoes of tears,
The weight of silence, the burden of fears.
Under the waves, the truth stirs awake,
Secrets emerge, for courage's sake.

In the still waters, reflections gleam,
Mirrors of moments, caught in a dream.
Hidden treasures await to be found,
Secrets beneath the surface abound.

As the tide turns, we face the blue,
Unlocking the depths, discovering new.
With every ripple, we learn to dive,
Secrets beneath the surface, alive.

Let the mysteries guide you below,
Where the heart yearns and the spirit will grow.
In the depths of being, so much to unveil,
Secrets beneath the surface prevail.

A Tangle of Dreams

In twilight's glow, our wishes blend,
A tangle of dreams that never end.
Colors swirl, painting the night,
A tapestry woven with light and delight.

Thoughts wander through starry skies,
Chasing the echoes of whispered sighs.
In the garden of hopes, our spirits fly,
A tangle of dreams, reaching high.

Each thread of desire, a vivid hue,
Intertwined destinies coming into view.
We gather our stories, each fragment gleams,
A collection of memories, a tangle of dreams.

As dawn approaches, the shadows fade,
Revealing the paths that we have made.
With every heartbeat, a rhythm extremes,
A symphony rising from our dreams.

Together we dance in the morning light,
Embracing the journey, taking flight.
In every twist, our hopes reclaim,
A joyful tapestry, a tangle of dreams.

Pathways of Emotion

In a forest deep, feelings roam,
Whispers of joy find a home.
Through laughter and tears, we weave,
In every heartbeat, we believe.

Sunshine flickers, shadows play,
Colors of heart in bright array.
Moments linger, softly they sigh,
Carrying dreams that never die.

Gentle streams flow through my thoughts,
In every drop, a lesson taught.
Roses bloom in fields of gray,
Hope emerges to light the way.

The sky reflects what's inside,
Every cloud, a truth to hide.
Emotions dance, a vibrant song,
In this journey, we belong.

Together we walk, hand in hand,
Crafting stories, love's command.
Through winding paths, we will find,
The strength that lives in heart and mind.

Shadows of Solitude

In the quiet night, whispers fade,
Lonely echoes softly invade.
Searching for warmth in the chill,
Yearning for contact, a heart to fill.

Moonlight drapes like a silver shroud,
Embracing silence, feeling proud.
Every corner holds a sigh,
In the dark, the shadows lie.

Images flicker, thoughts collide,
Solace found in the divide.
With each breath, a history shared,
In solitude, we are bared.

Time stretches, a thin thread spun,
Chasing after dreams undone.
Yet in stillness, light can seep,
Bringing peace where shadows creep.

Whispers haunt, but don't confine,
In solitude, we subtly shine.
A spark ignites, a flicker bright,
Breaking through the endless night.

Echoing Footsteps

Footsteps linger on the ground,
Each one tells a tale profound.
Through corridors of time we roam,
In every path, we find a home.

Silence pauses, I hear the past,
Moments echo, shadows cast.
In the stillness, memories sing,
Resonance of everything.

Steps of strangers brush my skin,
Each a journey hidden within.
Footprints wash on shores of sand,
Stories written by fate's hand.

The rhythm of life, a dance so sweet,
Guiding forward with each heartbeat.
In the echoes, we are led,
By the dreams that lie ahead.

From the past, we boldly stride,
Embracing change, never to hide.
With every beat, we form a chain,
Echoing footsteps in the rain.

The Riddle of Me

In mirrors cracked, reflections play,
Pieces of me, scattered away.
Searching deep, I find the clues,
In the shadows, I must choose.

Layers peel like fragile skin,
Each discovery, a spin within.
Questions linger, answers hide,
Waves of thought, I can't confide.

Fragments bright, yet some remain,
Lost in whispers, forged in pain.
Life's a puzzle, bits and parts,
Crafting tales from lonely hearts.

In every breath, a riddle grows,
Understanding as the river flows.
With each dawn, I draw the map,
Finding solace in the gap.

Embracing truth, I seek to be,
The one who's whole, the riddle of me.
In the journey, I will find,
The pieces woven, heart and mind.

Journeys within the Veil

In whispers soft the shadows creep,
Through dreams where hidden secrets sleep.
We wander paths of light and dark,
Searching for that sacred spark.

Beneath the stars, our spirits roam,
In realms where heart and mind call home.
Each step unfolds a tale untold,
As mysteries through time unfold.

The veil between is thin and frail,
Through it we weave, we set our sail.
With courage found in silent cries,
We seek the truth where darkness lies.

In every tear, a story flows,
In every smile, the journey grows.
With every whisper, we unveil,
The wisdom held within the veil.

So let us tread this path so deep,
Where souls connect and spirits leap.
Together here, our hearts align,
In journeys vast, our fates entwine.

The Hidden Compass

In silent woods where shadows play,
A compass lies to show the way.
Unseen, it guides with gentle hand,
Through realms of dreams and shifting sand.

When lost amidst the stormy night,
It whispers soft, igniting light.
Trust in the heart, it knows the way,
To lead you through the break of day.

With every beat, a map appears,
To navigate through doubts and fears.
The hidden compass, true and wise,
Reflects the depth within our eyes.

Seek not the path that's marked in stone,
For in the wild, you're not alone.
Each twist and turn, a chance to grow,
The compass spins to teach what's true.

So let it guide you through the haze,
To find the light, to mend your ways.
In journeys bold, you'll come to see,
The hidden paths that set you free.

Threads of Consciousness

In every thought, a thread appears,
Connecting dreams with hopes and fears.
We weave our lives on fabric wide,
In colors rich, in shades of pride.

The tapestry of heart and mind,
A nuanced dance of humankind.
Each moment threads a story true,
In every breath, a world anew.

With gentle hands, we pull and twist,
Creating beauty in the mist.
In laughter shared, in sorrows deep,
The threads we sew, through joy we leap.

Yet every thread can fray and break,
In trials faced, for love's own sake.
But in the weave, resilience shows,
The strength within as wisdom grows.

So savor every stitch you make,
For every choice, a path to take.
In consciousness, we find our role,
As threads unite the heart and soul.

Sculpting Shadows

With every breath, a shadow casts,
In silent forms, our moments last.
We shape the echoes of the past,
In shadows' dance, our stories vast.

The light reveals what's hidden near,
A sculpture born from hope and fear.
In voids we carve the dreams we seek,
A testament to hearts that speak.

From clay of doubt to stone of trust,
We mold ourselves, as we must.
Each figure tells a tale profound,
In shadows whispered, truths are found.

With every curve, a life takes form,
In shadows played, we weather storms.
Crafting visions where silence lies,
In art we find our sweet reprise.

So sculpt the shadows, give them breath,
In light, in dark, we conquer death.
Our stories told in shapes divine,
In shadows' grace, our souls align.

Reverberations of the Spirit

In twilight's glow, whispers call,
Echoes dance, weaves through the hall.
A sigh of hope, a breath of peace,
Waves of healing never cease.

Voices rise, a gentle hum,
In unity, we become one.
Carried forth on winds of change,
Love's embrace, our souls arrange.

Through shadows deep, a light appears,
Guiding hearts through doubts and fears.
In every heart, a sacred spark,
Illuminating paths through dark.

With each heartbeat, stories told,
Adventures of the brave and bold.
In reverberations, we find grace,
An endless dance, a timeless space.

Threads that Bind

In the fabric of our days,
We weave together in countless ways.
Threads of laughter, threads of tears,
Binding us through all our years.

Gold and silver, bright and bold,
Stories woven, dreams unfold.
In every stitch, a memory glows,
With every loop, our garden grows.

Through storms we weather, through calm we sail,
Interwoven lives, in heartfelt tale.
With every fray, we stitch anew,
Creating bonds, both strong and true.

In the tapestry of time,
Each thread a rhythm, each stitch a rhyme.
Together we rise, together we stand,
United in love, hand in hand.

The Cipher of the Mind

In shadows deep, thoughts entwine,
Riddles whispered, pure divine.
A puzzle locked, a secret kept,
In the heart of dreams, we've leapt.

Words like whispers, soft and clear,
Unlock the door, shed every fear.
In every silence, secrets grow,
A labyrinth where few may go.

Through corridors of memory's maze,
Find the light through the haze.
In riddles wrapped, the truth we seek,
Within the depths, the mind will speak.

Patterns dance, an intricate art,
Woven in the fabric of heart.
To decipher love, the truest clue,
Unlocking worlds, both old and new.

A Hidden Reverie

In quiet corners, dreams reside,
A hidden place where wishes hide.
Whispers soft as morning dew,
Echoes of what could be true.

Through the veil of time, we roam,
In the heart of night, we find home.
Secrets linger in tender light,
A dreamer's path takes graceful flight.

Beneath the stars, where visions play,
Lost in wonder, we drift away.
Captured moments, a fleeting glance,
In the hidden, we find our dance.

In shadows cast by hopes and fears,
We weave our tales through fleeting years.
In reverie, the spirit sings,
A world of wonder that dreaming brings.

The Subconscious Pathways

In shadows deep, the thoughts do weave,
Memories flicker, make us believe.
A labyrinth of whispers, soft and low,
Guiding our souls where few dare to go.

Dreams take flight on velvet nights,
Beneath the stars, unseen delights.
With every turn, the mind unlocks,
Secrets hidden in paradoxical clocks.

Clouded visions drift and play,
Through twilight worlds, they softly sway.
Chasing echoes of distant past,
In the silence, our fears are cast.

Gentle musings paint the night,
Drawing paths in fading light.
Seeking solace in the quiet,
Finding peace within the riot.

At last we learn to trust the way,
Through tangled thoughts, we boldly sway.
Each breath a step, each dream a guide,
In subconscious realms, we shall abide.

Fables of the Mind

Once upon a time, thoughts would roam,
Weaving tales in a silent dome.
Lost in fables, we chase the light,
In imaginations, hearts take flight.

A whispered story, aged and wise,
Unfolds like stars in midnight skies.
Each memory dances, a playful sprite,
Telling the truths hidden from sight.

In valleys deep, the fears reside,
Guarded closely, they seek to hide.
Yet gentle laughter breaks the spell,
In courage found, we rise and dwell.

Through pages turning, dreams long sought,
Live in the colors that visions wrought.
Let us gather the tales of old,
In the hearts of wanderers, boldly told.

With every chapter, wisdom grows,
In tangled fables, the heart knows.
Beyond the stories, we claim our part,
In the canvas of dreams, we share our art.

The Silent Wanderer

Through misty paths, the wanderer treads,
In silence profound, where stillness spreads.
Dreams are the lanterns guiding the way,
Illuminating souls, come what may.

With every step, the whispers call,
Echoing secrets, both great and small.
In the heart of night, the journey unfolds,
Stories of wonders the silence holds.

Shadows dance in the soft moonlight,
Cloaked in peace, the world feels right.
Carried by breezes, untouched and free,
Lost in the vastness, just me and me.

Reflections shimmer on water's skin,
Revealing the depths that lie within.
A gaze into stillness, the soul takes flight,
In the quiet embrace of the tranquil night.

The journey may twist, the path may wind,
Yet solace and truth are intertwined.
For in the silence, the wanderer finds,
The beating pulse of the open minds.

Reflections in Still Water

In a quiet pool, the world reflects,
Mirrored moments that nature protects.
Each gentle ripple disturbs the view,
Whispers of secrets, both old and new.

Colors merge in vibrant array,
Painting the echoes of the day.
Thoughts drift softly like leaves on stream,
Capturing fragments of a distant dream.

Beneath the surface, stories hide,
Bound by time, in silence they bide.
In the depths where shadows play,
Truths emerge in their own way.

Calm and clear, the water speaks,
To the wandering heart that seeks.
In tranquil depths, our visions bloom,
In the stillness, we find our room.

So pause awhile, let your thoughts flow,
In reflections deep, let your spirit grow.
For in still water, the soul will see,
The beauty of the journey, wild and free.

Light Beneath the Weight

In shadows deep, a flicker grows,
A gentle spark that softly glows.
Amidst the burden, hope takes flight,
A whispered promise in the night.

The heart's thrum beneath the strain,
A glimmer shouts through silent pain.
Each tear a prism, refracting light,
In darkest hours, we find our sight.

A heavy crown, yet head held high,
The weight of worlds, beneath the sky.
With every step, the light reveals,
A path of truth that gently heals.

In burdens shared, we find our peace,
Through unity, the weight will cease.
Together we rise, strong and bold,
With love as armor, hearts of gold.

So let the light, a guide, become,
Through trials faced, we will not succumb.
For every weight that life may skew,
Beneath its weight, the light shines through.

The Chiaroscuro of Emotions

In shadows cast by flickering flame,
The dance of feelings, never the same.
Joy mingles close with threads of despair,
In light and dark, we learn to care.

Sorrow's grip, a heavy hand,
Yet in its midst, we take our stand.
Through every hue, both bright and dim,
The art of life, an endless hymn.

A flicker there, a shadow here,
In every heartbeat, love draws near.
The contrast sharp, yet soft it flows,
In tangled webs, our essence glows.

Whispers rise from depths untold,
In silence wrapped, the truths unfold.
The chiaroscuro guides our way,
Through night and dawn, we find our sway.

In the canvas of our soul's refrain,
We paint our joy, embrace the pain.
For in the blend of light and shade,
The beauty of life is often laid.

Love's Enigmatic Footprints

In every step that you have tread,
A trace of love, where dreams are bred.
Soft whispers linger in the air,
With every heartbeat, a silent care.

The paths we crossed, like threads entwined,
In every silence, your voice defined.
Each look a promise, deep and clear,
The footprints echo, drawing near.

In twilight's glow, our shadows dance,
Two souls entwined in sacred chance.
With every breath, the world stands still,
Your love, a spark, igniting will.

Through shifting sands and paths unknown,
In love's embrace, we've brightly grown.
Each footprint left, a story told,
In every moment, our hearts unfold.

So let us wander, hand in hand,
Through fields of dreams, across the land.
For in each step, together we chase,
The enigmatic warmth of love's embrace.

Visions Behind Closed Eyes

In solitude, where silence reigns,
Behind these lids, imagination gains.
A world unfolds, both bright and vast,
Dreams take shape, as shadows cast.

Mountains rise and rivers flow,
In this realm, the heartbeats glow.
Colors swirl, dance without sound,
In quiet corners, joy is found.

Visions painted with every sigh,
In whispered thoughts, we learn to fly.
Behind closed eyes, the spirit roams,
In boundless realms, we find our homes.

Through laughter's echo and sorrow's thrall,
In every vision, we rise and fall.
Yet in the midst of night's embrace,
Hope's gentle light finds its place.

So close your eyes, let dreams take flight,
In shadows deep, you'll find the light.
For visions born in twilight's grace,
Reveal the magic, time can't erase.

Shadows in the Sanctuary

In quiet halls where whispers dwell,
Shadows dance and secrets tell.
Softly echoing the night,
Lost in dreams, obscured from sight.

Hallowed corners, silent plea,
Embrace the dark, set spirits free.
In gentle flickers, hopes ignite,
Guiding lost souls toward the light.

Candle flames, they flicker slow,
Casting shapes that come and go.
Ancient stones with stories steeped,
In the sanctuary, memories kept.

Beneath the arches, thoughts entwined,
Ethereal whispers, hearts aligned.
In every shadow, freedom found,
A sanctuary from the ground.

With each footfall, echoes roam,
The sanctuary, a sacred home.
In shadows deep, our spirits soar,
Forever held, forever more.

Inner Echoes

Beneath the calm, the currents churn,
Whispers rise from deep within.
A mirror shows what we discern,
Hidden fears and tales of sin.

Thoughts collide in tempest's grace,
Fragments flutter, quick to chase.
Each echo carries truth profound,
In silence, secrets can be found.

Mountains of doubt, rivers of hope,
In pondered depths, the heart will cope.
Waves of question, tides of time,
In inner echoes, life will rhyme.

Layers peeled, the soul laid bare,
Woven threads of love and care.
Resonating with each heartbeat,
Inner echoes, bittersweet.

Through shadows cast, clarity shines,
In every pulse the self defines.
Embrace the echoes, let them flow,
For in their depths, true wisdom grow.

Murmurs of the Unconscious

In twilight's glow, a whisper swells,
Unseen voices weave their spells.
Murmurs wrap the mind in night,
Beneath the surface, dreams take flight.

Echoes float on gentle streams,
Floating softly, tracing dreams.
In shadows cast by thoughts unchained,
The murmur stirs, the soul unpained.

Veils of slumber hide the truth,
Revealing all we felt in youth.
Wisps of memory guide the way,
Murmurs turn to light of day.

Fragments whisper, dance and play,
In the dark where dreams may sway.
From uncharted depths they rise,
Murmurs painting midnight skies.

To listen close is to embrace,
The silent pulse of time and space.
In every murmur, life will trace,
The echoes of the heart's own grace.

Maelstrom of Feelings

In the depths, a tempest brews,
Swirling colors, deepening hues.
Hearts in chaos, fierce and wild,
A maelstrom where hope is styled.

Tides of joy, floods of despair,
Caught in currents, unaware.
Rising waves of laughter, pain,
In this storm, everything's gained.

Whirlwinds toss the silent fears,
Dancing forth like forgotten years.
In every spin, a story spun,
In the maelstrom, we become one.

Tamed by fury, soothed in time,
We find rhythm, learn to rhyme.
From raging seas to calm repose,
The maelstrom of feelings flows.

Learning strength from tides that break,
Embracing all for love's own sake.
In every swirl, we rewrite fate,
Our hearts entwined, no time to wait.